Aisha Riaz is a young professional who is inspired from leaders around the world to write about organizational issues, employee empowerment, and to make a workplace better for employees. She has recently completed her CIPD studies after graduating from the American College of Dubai with a bachelor's degree in business. Born and raised in Dubai, she enjoys working in a multicultural environment as she believes that helps her learn different cultures and teachings.

This book is dedicated to all who wish to figure out what role they want to have in life, and how they can solve their problems on their own.

Aisha Riaz

IF WE COULD

Find the True Purpose in Our Work

AUSTIN MACAULEY PUBLISHERS™
LONDON • CAMBRIDGE • NEW YORK • SHARJAH

Copyright © Aisha Riaz 2022

The right of Aisha Riaz to be identified as author of this work has been asserted by the author in accordance with Federal Law No. (7) of UAE, Year 2002, Concerning Copyrights and Neighboring Rights.

All rights reserved. No part of this publication may be reproduced, stored in a retrieval system, or transmitted in any form or by any means, electronic, mechanical, photocopying, recording, or otherwise, without the prior permission of the publishers.

Any person who commits any unauthorized act in relation to this publication may be liable to legal prosecution and civil claims for damages.

The age group that matches the content of the books has been classified according to the age classification system issued by the Ministry of Culture and Youth.

ISBN – 9789948834731 – (Paperback)
ISBN – 9789948834748 – (E-Book)

Application Number: MC-10-01-7445866
Age Classification: E

First Published 2022
AUSTIN MACAULEY PUBLISHERS FZE
Sharjah Publishing City
P.O Box [519201]
Sharjah, UAE

www.austinmacauley.ae
+971 655 95 202

Table of Contents

Part 1   9

Accepting the Crowd's Response?

Part 2   15

Educating Others

Part 3   21

Is There a Problem?

Part 4   27

Can I Solve My Own Problem?

Part 5   33

Managers to Rethink About Their Roles

Part 6   39

Going Back to the Role of HR

Part 7   45

Moved On and Lost Talent

Part 8

Is the Termination Letter Ready?

Part 1
Accepting the Crowd's Response?

So how often did we just compromise on a decision when we were told that this is not how it is? You must be like THIS always. For everything has happened THIS way.

Why can't we change how we do our work?

Whenever you hear of organizational issues, you wish to have someone solve the problem. Either you are not able to explain yourself well or the concerned manager isn't ready to listen. You head to HR and they seem to be taking it to a hype for a couple of days and shutting down the case without any notice. Problems unresolved. Issues recurring. Employees resigning. Yet Business still RUNS!!! How???

Here, You and I are on one page. :)

Just like you, I wondered when will all this come to an END. Probably never, because no one seems to be bothered about it. Why, after all?

Sometimes, I felt I was wrong. Sometimes, I felt people must listen to my opinion just like I listen to theirs. Fair enough it should be this way. So to resolve, do I have to be an HR professional with some 12 years of experience? What if I knew more without any experience but rather knowledge through reading and observation and practicing too?

I was reading. Always. A habit that is always there. And so I started reading this too. Let me first understand what HR has to do with our issues. Then tell the solution. But first, I have to do a good study.

I looked for courses or rather some certifications or diplomas whatsoever. Few of them were just 4-day courses and to me it felt they were not enough. I don't think I can know what I want in just 4 days!

Alright, I spent 4 months looking out for the right course. I found CIPD. I searched some LinkedIn profiles. I looked through levels 3, 5, and 7. I kind of felt this was where I should be… So I took up the course but the study was not an ordinary one; at least, the one I was used to… I mean, last-minute study and assignment… You get it?

It made me do research and put down the links of all the information I was putting down in my assignments. This study did not just educate me about HR but I also felt it had made me more human.

A complete year's study changed my perspective of HR. I see it now as a department that has more responsibility, authority, and throughout the lifetime of the organization it has to be diligent. You see, it's not just an interview and landing a job through these guys. It's about your journey in the organization too. Every module made me reflect on my own experience at work. I wanted to tell people what was wrong and yes, here's a solution. Unfortunately, the restricted minds of theirs did not allow them to adapt to changes or any new opinions. They were happy with the way *things were going on in the company.*

There's even more. When our job applications are rejected, we are not told the reason. We kind of get an automated response; something like, "Unfortunately, XYZ has decided to move ahead in the selection process and your application is not considered at this time" etc.

Sometimes, they tell us at the last moment that we have lost our jobs. Things just change so quickly, as if it were a favor you had done hiring that employee in the first place.

Every time in my assignments, I shared my opinion too. I was discussing it with colleagues, friends, or whoever I knew. It showed that these were the people who actually got the issues I was talking about.

Looks like you are familiar with these situations. I am glad. Now, let's talk about the details!

===

Part 2
Educating Others

Overtime, I developed an interest in educating people about what I learned. When I applied for jobs, I was rejected because I had no relevant experience. I felt organizations were refraining themselves from providing training. I say I didn't stop there. I found my ways. I went to Instagram and started writing short posts. I asked questions, educated, did my study, and practiced.

While doing that, I was writing this book. Yes, the book you are reading *now*. I didn't take the diploma to get a job in HR. I had a larger perspective. I had a purpose. The purpose is what you'll understand once you have completed reading this book.

Why did I think of educating others when I wasn't someone with the experience of the HR professionals you have ever met? Because I wanted to tell you what I learned so you can learn from it too. I don't want you to be that ordinary HR who doesn't care about their role. Who have no idea what change they can bring if at all they take the step. But they don't because they are afraid of losing their jobs.

Fear makes you a coward.

I am not sure what's your perspective of them but I have mostly felt this: Organizations tend to impose rules without realizing what effects it will have or even if there is anything better that can be done.

Whenever I look at these top speakers or coaches or whoever becomes your inspiration, I notice they spend time learning and educating others. When we teach, we learn more. It's no fantasy that HR cannot be better, or it's just books. You feel it like that because people haven't really changed their minds to being better human beings. They just want to secure their jobs. I see books as sources of education. Remember, education is not just what you had at school or college. It's all your life to teach you how to live.

When I was posting on Instagram with very limited followers, like less than 50, including people from speaking different languages, I made sure my content was easy to understand. I asked questions to get their views/opinions, I shared my ideas, I shared what I felt makes sense and has logic.

And in this interaction, I was building knowledge. Whatever I knew so far was only a little part of it.

With no job, or no experience in HR, I didn't stop myself from doing what I wanted. And guess what. No one can stop me too. I felt as if there were no opportunities for me when looking at what my mind had inside it.

You see if you don't get an opportunity, you have to create one! That's right! You have to create one.

The opportunity I created had a thought that OK, I am not going to be ever allowed to do what I want, so rather than having a 9–6 job, I start with what I should. That's how it all started. Let me tell you just because I had around 50 followers at that time, I can assure you not everyone who read must have liked the posts. Read it again.

I pitched my training proposal to an organization, and was waiting every day to get a response. I was excited for what I wanted to do but that excitement was of no interest to them, it seemed. So should I have waited when I know I can write too?

===

Part 3
Is There a Problem?

What you know and I had known was all not even 1% of what HR does or should do. You see, the world's leading tech companies don't operate the way our ordinary businesses do. I would think to myself we are all aware of Apple but why don't our managers act like their managers would probably be doing? We are all not getting inspired. If we were, we would have acted upon it.

Most of us have concerns over timings. We want them to be flexible. Some days, we want an off but we are threatened for getting a day's pay deducted over doing such an act. There is great stress on making people achieve "numbers" without thinking or telling teams of ways that this can be achieved. Terminations have become a habit. Ignorance is at its peak.

What you must know is that termination is not a solution to your problem. The solution is working together with your employee to understand what's the issue they are facing at work. Get to know the REAL PROBLEM. Then solve it. I can't list down solutions.

And the internet can give you various ideas. But your problem needs your brain, not Google's search engine.

If I ask you how much have you invested in training your employees, you will reply back with the budget your finance department has allocated for it. The point here is not money but time. Did you actually see a difference after the training? Was it effective? Do all employees need training? Maybe someone just wants to tell you they have an idea of how things can be made better in your organization.

If I tell you to terminate an employee, oh you will gladly do that in a couple of minutes.

Hold on, did you change your mind because you read the first few pages that seemed so relevant to your life? OK. I am going to ask you again at the end of this book!

I feel that in the greed of earning more, we have somewhere lost the picture of humanity. We treat employees as if they were servants. We threaten them as if we were some powerful creature.

Looking at the problems you have at work today, write them down. If you don't know, find it out. Then begin writing. OK, with all the information that you have now, what are you planning to do about it?

How are you going to solve the problem? Who will you talk to? Is there anyone who can guide you about it?

So what can a man's mind do about its problem? Is every problem really a problem? Or is it just being perceived as a problem due to the challenges it has brought?

===

Part 4

Can I Solve My Own Problem?

Think about a problem that you currently have. Just one for now.

Can you think of how it all happened? Do not say it was being planned against you!

Well, let's say it's a work-related issue; since the book is about it, that's the perspective I will talk from. In the middle of the conversation, you were told that you haven't performed well at all! This sounds as if you were the worst employee in the organization.

Now, there are two sides.

One is your perspective – I know that I am not performing up to the standards. I know that I have to develop new skills but I need training and coaching probably. Or maybe, I am not able to perform because there are some issues in my mind, maybe a family problem, and so I cannot concentrate at work. Or maybe, you have a different idea of working, but that's not acceptable or appreciated at work.

Two; the Manager's perspective – This guy doesn't really want to work here. He's just taking up the salary and doing nothing, I see no results. I think it's time for him to leave the work forever. (I am not saying all managers are like this; of course, we all have our own opinions) or maybe, I have trained him enough, it's just that he is not interested in doing anything.

Quite common!

There's a simple way to solve this.

I have to fix my mind. Before I raise a question, I need to know what I do, the results it brings, and why my problems even exist.

Let's put my case here.

I have always wanted to do something purposeful at work. Something that brings a real change.

Something that makes the existing things better. So when I first started work, like everyone else I was concerned about learning as much as I can, spending as many hours as I can, and then coming home exhausted. In the first few years, I felt *Yeah, this is what you call work.* I was crazy about reading how to sell and bla bla bla. God, I think I read a lot about it. Then I began to practice and tried some ideas at my own work. And in the later years, I just felt nothing was making sense to me. I felt something was wrong.

Even though sometimes you are too good at what you do, but still it doesn't bring a satisfaction of purpose.

I figured out that people had a mindset so restricted to their own opinions that they could actually hear nothing you told.

Somewhere my ideas were working, yet they needed time. I was the only one with this new way of working. But maybe to people it sounded useless. So I thought it's time for me to not keep justifying or explaining people but rather trying to solve my own problems myself. And then I started with those Instagram posts I told you about and I started writing this book and I also was reading so I could continue my research and take an opportunity in the perfect time that Covid-19 had brought.

I know many people might curse Coronavirus for their problems, yet it has made us realize what's important and what's just temporary.

Now you see, though I kept applying for jobs, of course to support the own funds we require to live, I wasn't able to land any of those. I could feel the rejection before getting the rejection notification. You know why? Because I actually know what I want. And sorry, that's when things start turning away. You are walking out of the crowd and the crowd doesn't like it. So you can't complain and you can't blame anyone. All you can do is do what you want to do. And here, no more managers were telling me that I knew nothing!

So you see, we have to first analyze the problem. Is it because of myself and secondly, how can I solve it? In that case, I won't be wandering around blaming everyone, rather I would figure out a way and solve my own problem. Do I need anyone to solve it for me? The answer is NO. You can speak to people about it and get suggestions, but your problem is only solved when you act on a decision you have made about it. Otherwise, it stays there and piles up even more problems if left unresolved.

There's not a definite solution for everyone, as each one of us will have various situations and people that will be part of it and so you should be on your own to sort out your own problem.

===

Part 5
Managers to Rethink
About Their Roles

I haven't managed a team the way you are if you are actually the manager. You know how I see your role? One that is of guidance for his team.

You may ask yourself about your leadership style. Are you just a manager? That's not your role. Your role is to guide your employees. Your role is to learn from them and teach them too. Your role is to spend time with employees. Your role is not to look at that dashboard which tells you every minute how many sales calls have been made.

Your role is not to decide who to fire. Your role is to figure out why my team is not able to perform. 'Have I spent enough time with the person, have I provided the training and tools and the environment he requires to perform his job?' 'Have I fixed the timing so horrible that it doesn't suit him?' 'Am I the reason for the bad performance of my employees?'

Sometimes, managers are proud to say they manage a team of 40–50 employees but are you really managing? It's not the title on your business card or the salary that you earn or the big company you work for. It's about being human, one with heart and a brain. These two are great sources for any decisions that you make. So make your decisions wisely. You should be going the extra mile to solve problems. Go the extra mile to help people. Inspire them so they can inspire others. We need to be good. We don't always need to manage. Managing seems to be an ordinary word. That sounds like as if you are not really interested in your role to work with people rather just struggle to keep them together without building meaningful relationships.

Please don't feel hurt. Maybe your employees are trying to tell you this but they are scared. Just remember we have to make ourselves human beings and that's what we will always be. Our titles won't change our labels from homo sapiens. It will always stay in that category.

If you start practicing today, there's so much change you can bring in one quarter. Give it a try!

It's not difficult though to change yourself; it requires just one step! That's 'action'. When we act on what we have decided, we reach our goal. Even if you were to read a lot about changing yourself, unless you don't act on it, there's nothing happening in real. And so there stands a great challenge for us all.

If managers are to rethink their roles, then what is it that they have to change? It depends where you are now, what you do and what you must do and what you don't do that requires adjustments.

Start this by writing down what you do each day. Review it by the end of day and see what's the mess, what could be done instead.

===

Part 6
Going Back to the Role of HR

We know that this department will try to make both parties of an issue simply get over with the case and just work out a way to do anything better. Or sometimes, under the pressure from the boss, this department asks you to leave.

Of course, employees go to this department for their issues and soon realize that it's not worth their visit. Let me tell you as an HR professional you have a duty to your work. This is not about your usual work. This is about times when your assistance is required. It's actually a critical time. If you see the two parties don't get along, figure out why. Find out their interest, goals, and plans. Is termination a solution? Or do you see that the employee is more suited for another role at your company? Maybe you have a role for them. And maybe you don't. How about you create one, if possible?! Or refer them to someone you know who might require your employee's skills.

As an HR, don't be too excited to see someone's work experience and qualifications. You might find people interested in doing the work but not having any qualification at all. And you might find people with qualifications but no interest at all.

But what can you do for them in your own organization?

Isn't it starting from the recruitment process? You felt you finally got the guy and did all the process to ensure he gets the role. But what was in your mind? Your intention was the same as the organizational goals? Or was it to finish off with these interviews because it has taken quite many days to find the person you are looking for. And yet you still end up hiring the employee that may not be the right fit for your organization. Just a question, how do you figure out only within that interview if the candidate you have selected over the others is the right candidate for your business?

I would like to add up something important here. We often refrain from hiring talent that would require much training to develop both skills and knowledge for this role – the role may be critical for you but you never know what a fresher in this role can bring to your business. More than energy, its ideas that you are looking for and going to require for the business to step ahead in the process. If a business sticks to its own ideas all the time, I mean the idea of only one person, it's never going to make it to the top and in a few years may shut down too.

What made you think of hiring this employee? Have you settled down to hire this employee because you have a low budget and want that same candidate to do 3 employees' work at once. Did you make a mistake in your judgement? The CV/Resume looked great? Were you in a hurry? Were you tired that day? Did you just feel like putting the recruitment week to an end?

When you hired him, did you ensure he got enough support? Did he have the right start at work? It all begins from the recruitment process itself. And throughout that entire time till they settle down in their roles, they observe the organization. The start from their first day of work matters a lot. We call this onboarding and induction process. This is where the employees can judge how serious the organization is in hiring them. A fancy offer letter is not enough. Obviously, candidates are going to visit your website, check through your employees' profiles on LinkedIn and make a decision of working with you if at all. You have to ensure they have a good journey throughout their time with you. Isn't that linking to employee relations.

Do you think the guy who is heading the team is the right one? Should he be replaced? Does he need coaching too? Many times, we think that these "heads" do not know how to lead their teams. But that is just one perception of people who have had the experience.

No one is to be blamed. It is all what we do, and then we don't do that brings problems.

Each one of us needs to work on ourselves.

HR is the key department to any organization. When companies get bigger in terms of the employees they have, then many issues arise. However, if the policies and procedures are always updated and being practiced from the start, things don't get as messy as you see in your organizations today.

===

Part 7
Moved On and Lost Talent

Everyone who works for you won't stay with you forever. They will find new roles, better opportunities, better places, and better facilities and this tells them it's time to leave the current role and move on. Some organizations do not find this an issue. Massive hiring and firing employees is a routine. And rather they are used to doing the task.

I am sure you have seen or are aware of people who start working for their ex-employer's competitors. Now the competitors are making use of this great talent and now this employee of yours is performing in great numbers with them. So when he was with you, he was the least performing employee, with no interest in the job role and tasks assigned. It never made sense to him to do what he was told.

Do you ever wonder why this happens? It's not going to be about the pay every time, it may strongly be the environment too. The environment they may have is better than yours, but in terms of what? The facilities, the relationship with the line manager, the relationship with colleagues – who are available to help at any time, the growth options, and the training provided etc. You can provide all these too, only when you are concerned about the well-being of your employees. These days, everyone is concerned about having a better work environment, they are aware about the practices at various workplaces and so they won't be wasting a second staying with an employer that doesn't value their presence.

Yet, if these scenarios are common at your workplace, you must change the way things happen at your company. Your style is too old. Your processes are quite long and disturbed. Your policies have too many restrictions.

You see, there's so much within our own organizations that we have to improve, quite simple ideas on how you can make good use of the office space available. Look at the systems you have in place for the day-to-day business to happen. And most importantly, improve communication skills among yourself and your employees.

Communication practices that allow people to share ideas, give feedback and take necessary action to make work better and solve customer queries efficiently. And before you could solve customers' problems you have to solve employees' problems.

===

Part 8

Is the Termination Letter Ready?

This just made me laugh when I wrote it!

Coming to the end of writing this little book, with less but precise content, I wish to ask you:

If you are the manager at the moment, is there anyone you want to terminate? Have you got a justification for your decision?

If you are not the manager, but will be, are you going to be a unique guy who is concerned about employees rather than the benefits you receive from the numbers they achieve?

Your decisions should make the life of others better, not worse! Your decisions must set an example of a leader for the rest of your organization. Your decisions should inspire others to follow you and be much better!

Now let me ask, are you going to terminate him? (hahaha)

Listen up, we have to be *realistic*. Let's create no fantasy. Let's create no unnecessary issues. Let's give a thought on what we want in our life, figure out what we want from our work. What job role am I going to take? What kind of a boss am I really going to be able to work with? Which industry best suits my interest? Where can I build my career?

Let's bring out the real potential within ourselves of being the LEADER. Each one of you has this potential. You have to simply discover and start practicing.

It's time when organizations would prepare termination letters because they have to rush to the next recruiting batch, they look at what's going on around and analyze if termination would do any good.

What can rather be done, is discuss with your employee their interests, and place them in a role they would love to do and gladly work with you. No one today wants a "Work For You" role, they want a partnership.

And this partnership is going to help businesses thrive and make massive profits.

For those who do not wish to be employed will leave on their own. Termination Letters are of no more importance.

===

www.ingramcontent.com/pod-product-compliance
Lightning Source LLC
LaVergne TN
LVHW020437070425
807911LV00026B/533